THE STORY OF THE
Cornish Language

P. Berresford Ellis

TOR MARK PRESS · PENRYN

About the author

Peter Berresford Ellis, historian, literary biographer and novelist, has published 50 books to date under his own name and that of his pseudonym Peter Tremayne. An expert on Celtic history and culture, he is best known in Cornwall as the author of *The Cornish Language and its Literature* (Routledge & Kegan Paul, London, 1974) which is still regarded as the definitive history of the language and was a set text in the Cornish Language Board's examinations.

As 'Gwas-an-Geltyon' (Servant of the Celts) he is a bard of the Cornish Gorsedd. In 1985 he was appointed chairman of Scríf-Celt, the first ever Celtic languages book fair, at which over seventy Celtic language publishers exhibited. He was re-appointed chairman for the 1986 fair. In 1988 he was elected chairman of The Celtic League. He is also chairman of the London Association for Celtic Education.

His works range from *Caesar's Invasion of Britain* (Orbis, 1978) to *Celtic Inheritance* (Muller, 1985) and from *MacBeth: High King of Scotland 1040-57 AD* (Muller, 1980) to *A Dictionary of Irish Mythology* (Constable, 1987). He has lectured widely on aspects of Celtic history and culture both in the UK, Ireland, France and in the USA and Canada.

Other books in this series

Antiquities of the Cornish Countryside
Cornish Folklore
Cornish Legends
Cornish Mining — Underground
Cornish Recipes
Cornwall's Early Lifeboats
Cornwall's Engine Houses
Cornwall's Railways
Historic Houses, Castles and Gardens
Introducing Cornwall
Pebbles on Cornish Beaches
Shipwrecks Around Land's End
Shipwrecks Around the Lizard
The Story of Cornwall
The Story of Cornwall's Churches
The Story of St Ives
Surfing South-West
Tales of the Cornish Fishermen
Tales of the Cornish Miners
Tales of the Cornish Smugglers
Tales of the Cornish Wreckers
Twelve Walks on the Lizard
Victorian Cornwall

This second edition first published 1990 by
Tor Mark Press, Islington Wharf, Penryn, Cornwall TR10 8AT
© 1990 Tor Mark Press
ISBN 0-85025-310-1

The cover illustration reproduced by kind permission of
Paul Yockney, shows Dr John Chesterfield addressing the Cornish
Gorsedd at Poldhu, Mullion, in 1988 when he was installed as the
Grand Bard.

Printed in Great Britain by Swannack Brown & Co Ltd, Hull

1 The Cornish

In 1935 the British Broadcasting Corporation broadcast a programme of choral music from its Plymouth studio which caused feelings of surprise, puzzlement and interest among listeners. The programme of songs, given by the St Austell choir started off with a song called *Bro Goth agan Tasow*. Many thought they were listening to a Welsh programme until informed that they were listening to a programme of songs in the Cornish language. At once the BBC were flooded with requests for details. What was the Cornish language? Why was it different from English and so much like Welsh? Who, in fact, were the Cornish? So great was the response to the programme that it became a regular broadcasting feature. But as to the questions, few could answer them clearly for, apart from a few learned theses tucked away in academic journals, little information was generally available.

The Cornish are the second smallest of the six Celtic nationalities — the Irish, Manx and Scots (Goidelic Celts) and the Welsh, Bretons and Cornish (Brythonic Celts). The Cornish were the first Celtic nation to 'lose' their language, the last people with native knowledge of the language dying in the nineteenth century.

In 1974 the last native-speaker of Manx (Ned Maddrell) died. The 1971 Census had listed 284 Manx-speakers but, with the exception of Ned, they were revivalists. Manx became the second Celtic language to die as a generally spoken language in modern times.

The other Celtic countries have managed to retain a corpus of native speakers. In Ireland (the 26 County state) the 1981 Census showed 31.6% of the population (1,018,312) as Irish-speaking. Since Partition, no figures are issued for the Six Counties although it has been announced that Irish-speakers there will be enumerated in the 1991 Census and this is expected to be a substantial figure. In Scotland only 1.6% of the population (79,307) were accepted by the 1981 Census as Scottish Gaelic-speaking. A further 3,313 speakers were disqualified as it was maintained they had learnt the language and were not 'native speakers'. In Wales 18.9% of the population (503,549) were given as Welsh-speaking in 1981. The French do not issue figures but it was estimated that there are currently 800,000 Breton-speakers. These figures do not include the considerable number of Celtic speakers domiciled outside the Celtic countries.

These Celtic nationalities are all that is left of an ancient civilisation which left its mark from Asia Minor to Ireland.

The Celts were the first Trans-Alpine people to emerge into

3

recorded history, originating, according to ancient chroniclers, from the region round the Lower Danube. They invaded and settled in Italy at the beginning of the third century BC and sacked Rome itself in 387-386 BC. Polybius tells us that the Romans remained under Celtic domination until 349 BC when they rose against their conquerors and by 345 BC the Celtic conquest had been turned back. However, the Celts remained in Italy as settlers down to imperial times. Evidence of their settlement is shown in such place names in northern Italy as Trevi, Treviso, Treviglio, the River Trebia etc. A comparison with some Cornish place names is interesting.

In the next century the Celts turned towards Greece and in a spectacular campaign destroyed the armies of Macedonia, Haemos and Thessaly. Finally they defeated an Athenian army at Thermopylae before flooding through the gorges of Parnassos to sack the great temples of Delphi in 279 BC. Although the Greeks finally turned back this Celtic invasion, Thrace remained a Celtic kingdom until 193 BC. Some Celts pushed into Asia Minor and established a state called Galatia. Henri Hubert in *The Greatness and Decline of the Celts* points out: 'What we know of the Galatian state gives us our first example of the organisation of a Celtic state'. What is astonishing is the intrinsic democratic character of Galatia, a state referred to by the chroniclers as the Commonwealth of the Galatians. Government was by an assembly of 300 elected representatives and Galatia remained a Celtic speaking country up to the fifth century AD.

Of the early Celtic civilisation, the druids as philosophers, exponents of the Celtic religion and natural scientists, were well known and respected in the ancient world. The religion was one of the first to evolve a doctrine of immortality. Druids taught that death is only a changing of place and that life goes on with its forms and goods in another world, a world of the dead which gives up living men. Therefore a constant exchange of souls takes place between the two worlds . . . death in this world brings a soul to the other and death in the other world brings a soul to this one. Julius Caesar observed that this religious outlook could have accounted for the reckless bravery of the Celts in battle, with their apparently complete lack of any fear of death. As to the philosophies of the druids, Aristotle, Sotion and Clement all state that early Greek philosophers had borrowed much of their philosophy from the Celts.

Cicero comments that the druids were great natural scientists who had knowledge of physics and astronomy applied in the construction of calendars. The earliest known Celtic calendar dates from the first century AD and is far more elaborate than the rudimentary Julian one. This is the *Calendrier de Coligny* now in the Palais des Arts, in Lyons.

It is also by far the oldest extensive document in a Celtic language.

Of the Celtic languages, Irish takes its place in history as the third classical language of Europe, following Greek and Latin. Although Irish became the third written language of Europe, as Professor Calvert Watkins of Harvard also points out, 'Irish has the oldest *vernacular* literature of Europe.' Both Irish and Welsh early Celtic literatures contain an enormous wealth of mythology and poetry. HM and NK Chadwick in *The Growth of Literature* sadly point out: 'The Celtic literatures are practically unknown, except to persons who have spoken the languages from childhood. A few adaptations of early Irish sagas have recently had a certain vogue; but it may safely be said that very few people in this country have any conception of the extent and value of early Irish literature . . . The early Celtic literatures should not be ignored as they are at present.'

This then was the civilisation from which the Cornish sprang. The Celts began to invade Britain in the first millenium BC and, at the time of the Roman Conquest, 43 AD, Britain was entirely Brythonic or British-speaking. The Romans settled mainly in south-eastern Britain, halting at Exeter and leaving Cornwall more or less to itself. Similarly, they did not conquer Wales or Scotland, though not from any want of trying. Among the Celts of central and eastern Britain, Latin mingled with the Celtic speech. In the fifth century the Roman occupation ended and fierce Saxon hordes began to invade. In the fifth and sixth centuries, in the face of these invasions, large groups of Brythonic Celts migrated to Europe, many seeking asylum in a peninsula called Armorica. They took with them the name of their country and we know Armorica today as Brittany, or little Britain. Their language at the time of migration was exactly the same as Cornish and Welsh. Today, Breton is closer to Cornish than to the latter. Other Brythonic Celts settled in Galicia, in northern Spain where, by the tenth century, they had become absorbed.

The remaining British Celts occupied western Britain; from Cornwall and Devon, their settlements extended through Wales to Cumberland and into Scotland, where they mingled with the Goidelic Celts. In the face of the Saxon onslaught the Celts formed an alliance. But, after nearly two centuries of struggle, the Celtic leader, Penda, was defeated by the 'Englishman' Oswy at the battle of Winwaed Field in AD 655. This was the last time the Celts seriously contended with the English for supremacy in the isle of Britain. The 'weahlas' or 'foreigners', as the Saxons called the Celts, became split into three groups and separated from each other, the main body being driven into the mountainous west. There they formed an independent country which the Saxons called 'the land of foreigners' or Wales (weahlas) but which the Welsh called Cymru or 'the land of comrades'.

In Northern Britain another country called Cymru was formed but this small kingdom of Cymru (pronounced Cum-ree) was incorporated as part of the Celtic kingdom of Scotland in the eleventh century. By the end of the following century, the Scottish ruler Callum a' chin mhor (the slayer of MacBeth) was defeated by the English and had to surrender his kingdom to England as the price of defeat. The English retained the ancient name of Cymru in the Anglicised form of Cumbria and Cumberland. Although the Celtic language soon ceased to be spoken, Cumberland is still full of Celtic place names whilst the peculiar style of Cumberland wrestling is remarkably similar to that in Cornwall.

In the south-west of Britain, the Celts of Devon and Cornwall united into the kingdom of Dumnonia but its eastern border was weak and slowly the Saxons began to move into Devon. Within a few years Dumnonia had disintegrated and the Celts were confined in the kingdom of Kernow, which the English called 'the land of the Cornish foreigners' — Cornu-weahlas or Cornwall. Being on the western side of the Tamar this was less accessible to the invaders.

As a result of the geographical separation imposed upon the various groups of Brythonic Celts, differentiations began to emerge in their languages. Breton had its own growth while the Brythons of Cumbria were, by the eleventh century, swamped by Scottish gaelic and English. In Wales the language began to flourish as a vehicle for a rich literature, although the first recorded poetry composed in 'Welsh' was written in Scotland. The sixth century Aneirin was a poet attached to the court of Mynyddawg Mwynvawr, king of the Gododdin whose capital was at Eiddin (Edinburgh). Also from the sixth century Taliesin and Llywarch Hen were from southern Scotland. The language of these poets was, at this time, exactly the same as Cornish.

It is not until the ninth century that we have the first recorded words of a language which can safely be recognised as Cornish.

2 The Conquest of Cornwall

Little is known about Cornwall during the period of history known as the Dark Ages. Confusion has been created by the failure of the ancient historians to distinguish clearly between the kingdom of Kernow (Cornwall) and that of Kernev (Cornouaille, Brittany). Christianity prospered and shadowy figures of saints and kings played their part in its history. Between AD 450 and AD 550 Christian missionaries from Ireland and Wales came to Cornwall leaving behind, as their memorials, saintly place-names such as St Columb, St Ives, St Mawgan, St Tudy and St Mabyn. The Irish missionaries, moreover, left memorial inscriptions in Ogham, the early form of Goidelic Celtic script.

Although the Romans did not occupy Cornwall as intensively as they did other parts of Britain, they, too, left traces of their activities, including several inscribed milestones. The native Cornish chieftains, during or immediately after the Roman occupation, were commemorated by numerous Christian memorial stones, inscribed in often indifferent Latin. Two of these stones, moreover, are inscribed in both Latin and the Ogham script. One of the oldest of the memorials of this period is called Men Scryfa—the written stone—which stands on the granite uplands of the Land's End peninsula. The inscription reads RIALOBRANI CUNOVALI FILI—Rialobran son of Cunoval. Near St Cleer on Bodmin Moor, there are two cross bases carved in Irish style, the larger bearing the words DONIERT RIGAVIT PRO ANIMA—Doniert ordered (this cross) for (the good of) his soul. Doniert was the Cornish king Dungarth who was accidentally drowned in AD 878. A cross outside Penlee House in Penzance bears the inscription REGIS RICATI CRUX, dated to the tenth century. This is the cross of Ricatus, another Cornish ruler.

Perhaps the most romantic of these memorials stands at a cross roads near Fowey, not far from the earthworks of Castle Dore, the fortress of King Mark, whose bride Iseult was escorted from Ireland by Tristan, later to become her lover. The inscription reads DRUSTANUS IC IACIT CUNMORI FILIUS. In the ancient manuscript, *The Life of St Pol de Leon,* we are told that Mark, who ruled Cornwall between AD 570 and AD 585 was named Marcus Quonomorus. Tristan could be a corruption of the Celtic name Drustan. This then, could be the actual memorial to Tristan, son (not nephew) of King Mark of Cornwall.

One of the earliest manuscripts of the Tristan and Iseult romance was written by Florence of Worcester (died AD 1118) but Professor J Loth in his famous study of the romance claimed the original version in Cornish went to France via Brittany and there French poets adapted the story. These versions were written in the latter half of the twelfth century. Strangely enough it was from France that the romance made its way back into Cornish literature, ASD Smith (Caradar) translated one edition, *Le Roman de Tristan et Iseult,* back into modern Cornish, *Trystan hag Ysolt,* published in 1951. It was this romance that inspired the composer Franz Liszt to write his celebrated *Cornish Rhapsody* and Wagner to write the opera *Tristan und Isolde* while other composers have based operas on it.

By the seventh century Dumnonia had dissolved and Saxons were pushing westward. By the eighth century, Cynewulf and his men were bold enough to forage into north-east Cornwall but the Saxons were soundly defeated by the Cornish at Camel in AD 721-722, but the weight of numbers was against the Cornish. In AD 825 the latter fought a great battle in Devon and a few years later, realising their precarious position, they enlisted the help of the Danes. The subsequent battle fought at Hingston Down, east of Callington, resulted in a Cornish defeat. However, it was not until the year AD 936 that Athelstan, king of Wessex (925-940), drove the Cornish out of Exeter and defeated Hywel, the last independent king of Cornwall. Athelstan fixed the River Tamar as the boundary between his Saxon kingdom and 'the west wealhas'. Cornwall was, in fact, marked on maps as 'West Wales' until as late as the seventeenth century. In spite of the boundary that he had fixed, the Saxon king did not allow the Cornish an independent existence.

He started to eradicate the Celtic culture as a 'reform' and in this way remodelled Celtic monastic centres of learning along Saxon lines. It can safely be supposed that, in doing so, Athelstan destroyed a great many early Cornish manuscripts, accounting for the sad lack of literature from this period. Perhaps the original Tristan and Iseult tales were destroyed in this fashion. The Saxons also made St Germans the seat of the bishopric of Cornwall. It had been the seat of a Cornish bishop since AD 429. This bishopric was transferred to Crediton in 1043 and then to Exeter. Not until the nineteenth century did Cornwall have its own bishop once more.

It was during the struggle against Saxon domination that the legend of Arthur was born. If he existed in fact, he was certainly a Cornish ruler who opposed conquest by the Saxons. The first version of this legend that has survived was written by the Welshman, Geoffrey of Monmouth, in the twelfth century. He states that Arthur's birthplace was Tintagel, formerly Trevena. Experts have identified various sites in Cornwall with places in the early versions of the legend. It was, of course, thirteenth and fourteenth century writers who embellished the legend with tales of medieval knighthood and chivalry.

At the time of the Norman conquest in 1066, Cornwall was an earldom held by one Cadoc, obviously a native Cornishman. His arms were 'a black shield with golden bosses or roundals', which is the present coat-of-arms of the Duchy. It would seem, therefore, that Cornwall was still faily independent of the Saxons at this period. The Domesday Book shows that the Normans settled in Cornwall as baronial landowners. Speaking Norman-French, they interfered little with the Cornish language. The Saxons, however, were placed in the position of a middle class and their treatment of the native Cornish increased in severity because of their position.

From the post-Conquest period onwards we begin to have more extensive examples of written Cornish, although perhaps the earliest work which recorded it as a written language was a tenth century manuscript *The Bodmin Gospels Manumission.* This work records many Cornish names and words. The earliest authoritative work on the language is the twelfth century Cottonian Vocabulary, also in the British Museum. This contains seven pages of Cornish nouns, covering parts of the human body, birds, beasts, fishes, trees, herbs, ecclesiastical and liturgical terms plus a number of adjectives. Preceding the vocabulary is a calendar containing many other Cornish words.

A twelfth century story in Latin written by John of Cornwall shows us how much pre-Conquest literature must have been lost. The manuscript — *The Prophecy of Merlin* — was translated by him from a very early Cornish manuscript. In this version he attaches notes which gives some passages in the original Cornish. The only known manuscript of his work that survives, a fourteenth century copy, is in the Vatican Library in Rome.

In the Register of John de Grandisson, Bishop of Exeter (1327-69), there is recorded a dispute in the parish of St Buryan, four miles from Land's End. Formal submissions were made in French by thirteen prominent 'middle class' parishioners, while the rest of the evidence was given in Cornish and translated by one Henry Marseley, rector of St Just. After this hearing, the bishop preached a sermon which then translated into Cornish by Marseley. Writing some time later, de Grandisson remarked on the fact that an ancient British tongue was still spoken in 'extremis Cornubie'. De Grandisson, it appears, was very conscious of his rôle as administrator of the Christian doctrine. Certain English priests preached to monoglot Cornish and Welshmen in Latin, French or English only, so if their congregations wished to hear the teachings of the Church they were obliged to learn those languages. In 1339, however, a licence was granted to J Polmarke to help the vicar of St Merryn, near Padstow, 'expound the Word of God in the said church in the Cornish language'. In a list of penitentiaries for the archdeaconry of Cornwall, dated 1335, Brother Roger of Truro was licensed to preach in Cornish and Brother John of Bodmin to preach in Cornish and English.

Meanwhile, in England itself a fierce linguistic struggle was taking place. Following the Norman Conquest, Norman French had become the language of the country and, according to Mario Pei in *Story of the English Language* 'the speech of the conquered was banned from all polite society and official usage, it was despised as the jargon of peasants and practically ceased to be a written language'. English, in fact, was a dying language.

By the beginning of the fourteenth century, a movement seeking to gain official status for English, had arisen in the country. The growing support it received brought several reactions from the authorities. In 1332 an Act of Parliament decreed that French must be taught to all children receiving education and in 1325 at Oxford it was decreed all conversations in the city should be in Latin or French. From the Cornish viewpoint, the irony of this English language movement was the fact that it was led by Cornishmen.

One of them was John Trevisa from St Mellion, a Cornish-speaking cleric who gave the English the biggest encyclopaedia and history of the day in their own veracular. Trevisa died in 1402. Writing about the change from French to English, he states: 'John of Cornwall, a grammar master, changed the instruction and construing in the grammar schools from French into English: and Richard Pencrych learned that kind of teaching from him and other men from Pencrych, so that now, in the year of Our Lord, 1385, the ninth of the second King Richard after the Conquest, in all the grammar schools of England, children are now dropping French and construing and learning English'. Basil Cottle in *The Triumph of English 1340-1400* writes: '. . . we are asked to believe, by a Cornishman, with a Cornish name, that two others from his Duchy were largely responsible for the redemption of what wasn't even their native tongue, since all three must have been originally Celtic speaking'.

In 1349 it was permissible to teach English in schools; in 1362 pleas to Law Courts were acceptable in English and not, as before, only in French or Latin, and in 1362 also, members of parliament were allowed to debate in English. The final step was in 1413, when English became the official language of the royal court. While three Cornish speaking Cornishmen had saved the English language from death, they had, in fact, dealt a blow at the continuance of their own language.

In east Cornwall more Cornishmen began to adopt English, which had now replaced Norman French as the language of the ruling classes. The lesser gentry were quick to follow and thus only the poorer classes continued to speak solely Cornish. In court records it can be seen that translators had to be employed whenever necessary. The position of the language by the end of the fourteenth century, in the face of the conquest, was still strong. In north-east Cornwall English was spoken but in most of the south-east the people were mainly bi-lingual—and when a people are bi-lingual they usually begin to drop the language which has no commercial value. Only in the west of the peninsula did the Cornish remain entirely monoglot.

3 Middle Cornish

Until the reign of Henry VIII there is no really reliable knowledge as to the state of the Cornish language. By this time it had become transformed from the harsh Old Cornish into a softer sounding tongue, today termed Middle Cornish. That the language was reaching its highest development may be seen from the extent of literature left us from fifteenth and sixteenth century manuscripts. This literature is in the form of poetry and religious plays which were acted in the open air in various parts of the Duchy. The object of these plays was to teach the Cornish people, by means of visual representation as well as verse, the stories of the Bible.

During this time Bibles were available only in Latin or English and those who only knew Cornish had to learn either of those languages to read the scriptures. Perhaps the authors of these plays used them as a medium to teach the messages of the Bible without undertaking the mammoth task of producing a Bible in Cornish, as was done with Welsh and Irish. According to the Cornish scholar, A S D Smith, 'the mature Cornish in which the plays are written can only be the outcome of a long tradition of Cornish writing'. The plays served not only to give religious instruction but to rally people to their mother tongue and to keep the language alive in the face of pressure from English.

The Wars of the Roses (1455-1485) added yet another pressure on Cornish as a language, despite the geographical remoteness of the south-west peninsula. Many of the county's gentry took part in the wars and were killed or had their property confiscated by the victors; new families moved into Cornwall and were not content to let their labourers continue speaking Cornish. Cornish speakers began to feel their 'lowly' position. To be a gentleman one had to be English and everyone aspired to be a gentleman.

The great Renaissance of Learning and the invention of the printing press did little or nothing for Cornish. Learning was passed on through the medium of English alone and nothing was printed in Cornish, the language being looked upon simply as a rustic dialect . . . the speech of the poor and the ignorant.

The religious plays, however, were a bulwark against the complete erosion of the language. These plays, some taking three days to perform, were enacted at the village amphitheatre or *plen an gwary* at the time of a religious festival. Such an amphitheatre can be seen in Bank Square, St Just-in-Penwith, seven miles from Penzance. One of the earliest of these works is *Pascon agan Arluth,* a versified narrative of the events of the Passion of Christ. The earliest known copy is a fifteenth century one, said to be the original which was found in the church at Sancreed.

The biggest work of this period if the *Ordinalia* — an extremely lengthy three part drama said to have originated from Glasney Priory about 1450. The first play of this trilogy is called *Origo Mundi* — the Creation of the World; the second play is *Passio Domini,* showing the events leading to the Crucifixion of Christ while the third play is *Resurrectio Domini* showing the Resurrection, Ascension and even the death of Pontius Pilate.

The most interesting piece of literature, however, is *Bewnans Meryasek* — the life of St Meriasek or Meriadoc, the Bishop of Vannes, in Brittany, who became a missionary in Cornwall and the patron saint of Camborne. This is the only full length saint's play to survive in a British language. It was written for performance over a two day period at a Camborne festival and it is interesting to note that Meriasek's name survived until recently in the nickname used for Camborne people — 'merra-jeeks' or 'merry sticks'. The first manuscript of this play was written by a priest named Radulphus Ton in 1504. It is significant to note that the rector of Camborne in 1504 was John Nans who had previously been Provost of Glasney, Penryn, where most of the Middle Cornish dramas were written. *Bewnans Meryasek* was unknown until 1869 when the manuscript was discovered by chance by the Cornish scholar Robert Williams.

The Reformation, starting in 1533, was the turning point against those who had struggled to keep Cornish alive. During the reign of Henry VIII, Andrew Borde had written in his *Boke of the Introduction of Knowledge,* published in 1542, that: 'In Cornwall is two speches, the one is naughty Englysshe, and the other is Cornysshe speche. And there be many men and women the which cannot speake one word of Englysshe but all Cornysshe.' The position of the language at the beginning of the Reformation is clear from this statement.

In 1547 Edward VI decreed that *The English Book of Common Prayer* should be introduced into Cornwall. Old Celtic customs adapted by the Catholic Church were to be stamped out. It was recorded that Dr John Moreman, rector of Menheniot, was the first to introduce the English language into church services in 1540. R Polwhele (*History of Cornwall*) comments: 'If the inhabitants of Menhenniet [*sic*] then, in the East of Cornwall, were not acquainted even with the Lord's Prayer in English before they were instructed by their vicar, it may well be supposed that further West, the people had still less knowledge of English.' King's Commissioners were sent to enforce this new legislation in Cornwall. One of them, attempting to remove religious statues from Helston parish church in typically ruthless fashion, was stabbed to death. Feelings grew extremely bitter and the following year, for the third time since the Norman Conquest, a Cornish force was raised to defend the rights of Cornishmen. An army of 6000 prepared to march across the River Tamar, led by Humphrey Arundell of Lanherne and Henry Boyer, Mayor of Bodmin.

At first they sent a petition to the young king and, although professing their loyalty, simply stated 'We will not receyve the new service'. Among the reasons given, one states significantly, 'we, the Cornyshe men, whereof certain of us understande no Englyshe, utterly refuse thys newe Service'. Lake (*Parochial History of Cornwall*) comments: 'The Cornishmen in this rebellion were probably as much instigated by the attempt of the government to displace the old language in the service of the church as by the other innovations made upon their religion'. Edward answered this petition in what was considered an unsatisfactory manner and the Cornish army marched across the Tamar into Devon and laid siege to Exeter.

These were the sons of Cornishmen who, in 1496, had marched with Michael Joseph An Gof of St Keverne and Thomas Flamanck of Bodmin all the way to Blackheath in Kent before their army was defeated. An Gof ('The Smith') was executed at Tyburn in London. The reason for the insurrection was that the Cornish refused to pay taxes to supply arms for a war against their fellow Celts of Scotland. After their defeat at Blackheath, the Cornish again marched in 1497 under the banner of the Pretender Perkin Warbeck, in alliance with Scotland. They again suffered defeat.

Like their fathers before them, the Cornishmen of 1548 were defeated by superior numbers but, in the words of one who fought against them, only after a display of such 'valour and stoutness he never, in all the wars he had been in, did know the like'. With the Cornish army routed, its leaders were soon rounded up and executed. English was thereafter enforced on the Cornish in all religious and civil matters. John Whitaker (*Ancient Cathedral of Cornwall,* 1804) stated: 'English too was not desired by the Cornish, as vulgar history says and as Dr Borlase avers, but, as the case shews itself plainly to be, was forced upon Cornwall by the tyranny of England, at a time when the English language was yet unknown in Cornwall. This act of tyranny was at once gross barbarity to the Cornish people, and a death blow to the Cornish language'.

Had the new prayer book and Bible been translated into Cornish as they were into Welsh it may be wondered whether the language would have survived longer than it did. It is true that a Protestant movement tried to remedy the matter in 1560 by petitioning that 'it may be lawful for such Welsh or Cornish children as can speake no Englishe to learn the Praemise in the Welsh tongue or Cornish language'. But this petition was refused.

The persecution of Catholics at this time ended the centuries-old intercourse between Cornwall and Brittany. Bretons had been living freely among their fellow Celts in Cornwall — as can be seen from parish registers and Lay Subsidy Rolls — but, after 1560, their names cease. The idea of capitalising on the persecution of Catholics amongst the religious Cornish occurred to an Italian agent of Philip II of Spain. This agent wrote to Philip (a letter now in the Spanish State Papers of the British Museum) pointing out that like the Irish, the Cornish were Catholics and a different race with a different language and customs from the English. The Italian agent thought the Cornish would be likely to help Catholic Spain in their wars against Protestant England.

Following the subjugation of Cornwall, the Cornish language was derided as a mere dialect by playwrights. In 1550 a play appeared entitled *The Image of Idleness . . . translated out of the Troyance or Cornyshe tongue by Olyver Old Wanton.* This play, a second edition of which appeared in 1574, derides the language and includes some Cornish in it.

By the start of the seventeenth century there were only a few monoglot Cornish speakers left, mostly in the extreme west from St Ives to Ludgvan, Zennor and Land's End. Most of eastern Cornwall spoke only English, while the rest of the Duchy was bilingual.

4   The Cornish Scholars

The seventeenth century saw a rapid deterioration of the language as an everyday form of speech. By the end of the century Cornish speakers remained only in the extreme west of the peninsula. Because the ultimate death of the language was foreseen, a group of scholars banded together in the latter half of the century and began to make a study of it and its literature. This period can well be called the period of Cornish scholarship. Writing at the beginning of the century, however, Richard Carew in his *Survey of Cornwall* (1602) stated that the majority of Cornish were bilingual. He also noted that the *plen an gwary* plays still attracted large audiences.

In *Speculum Magnae Britanniae pars Cornwall* (1610), the author, John Norden addresses himself to King James I and explains the relationship of the Cornish to the Welsh, pointing out that the Cornish 'retayned the British speache uncorrupted as theirs of Wales is'. Cornish, he maintained, was far easier to pronounce. He states: 'And yet (which is to be marveyled) though the husband and wife, parents and children, masters and servants, do naturally communicate in their native language yet there is none of them in a manner but able to converse with a stranger in the English tongue, unless it be some obscure people who seldom confer with the better sort. But it seemeth, however, that in a few years the Cornish will be, by little and little, abandoned'.

The English Civil War of 1642-46 uprooted many Cornishmen and, with the two armies camped across Cornwall, inroads were again made on the language. With the Royalist army of Cornwall was a young lawyer from Essex, whose diary gives us a very clear picture of the situation of the language. The lawyer, Richard Symonds who was born in 1617, kept a detailed diary of 1644 (now in the British Museum) and in it he records that 'all beyond Truro they speak the Cornish language' and he adds 'at Land's End they speak no English'. Symonds also jotted down a list of common words in Cornish and four short conversational sentences.

The only major piece of Cornish literature written during this period that survives is a play called *Gwryans an Bys* — The Creation of the World — written by William Jordan of Helston in 1611. It is based on the *Origo Mundi* drama and, in fact, Jordan borrowed passages from it.

Scholars were not optimistic over the future of the Cornish language. John Ray prophesied in his *Itinerary* (1662 and 1667) that 'the language is like in a short time to be lost'. Visiting St Just in 1667, Ray claimed a Dickan Gwyn of that parish was the only man he could find who could write Cornish, although he also claims a man called Pendarvis had more scholastic knowledge of the language.

William Scawen in *Antiquities Cornu-Britannica* (*circa* 1680), gave a number of reasons why the language was declining. He lists the places where the language was still spoken and remarks that the vicar of Landewednack at the Lizard had to preach in Cornish until 1678, when he was replaced. Cornish, Scawen states, was the only language which the people of the western promontories of Meneage and Penwith (that is, the Lizard and Land's End) knew. Among the reasons he gives for the decline were lack of literature; loss of intercourse between Brittany and Cornwall; loss of legends and ancient records; indifference of the Cornish about their heritage; no church services in Cornish; and the cessation of the religious plays.

In the late seventeenth century scholars in the neighbourhood of

Penzance formed a group to preserve and further the language. These were led by John Keigwin of Mousehole (1641-1710) who was a master of Latin, Greek, Hebrew, French and Cornish. Among the group of active scholars were William Gwavas, John and Thomas Boson, Thomas Tonkin and Oliver Pender, all of whom have contributed much to the language. It was these scholars who attempted to translate essential parts of the Bible into Cornish in order to revive popular interest through religion. Unfortunately it proved too great a task although Keigwin and John Boson managed to translate *Genesis.* The work was furthered by a William Rowe of Sancreed, who used Wella Kerew or Willow Kerewe as a pen name.

Keigwin and his group concentrated on translating various passages of the Scriptures, proverbs and colloquial sentences. They also translated songs popular at the time. Keigwin also revised *Pascon agan Arluth, Origo Mundi* and *Resurrectio Domini,* as well as translating a letter written by Charles I, in 1643, thanking the people of Cornwall for their help against Parliament. The complete Bible in Cornish did not materialise, though *Brice's Weekly Journal* (Exeter) states in 1727: 'And I hear of a gentleman in Cornwall ... who has taken noble mighty pains in translating the Bible into Cornish or Cornubian Welsh'.

John and Thomas Boson left behind them a great deal of Cornish Literature, but much of the credit given to them should really go to their father, Nicholas Boson of Newlyn. Nicholas was a native speaker of Cornish, having acquired his knowledge without making any academic study of the language. He had brought up his three children, John, Thomas and Katherine, as native Cornish speakers but he made them study the language academically as well. The writings of the Bosons, especially that attributed to John (born in 1655) have become of great value to Cornish scholars. In 1700 he published *Nebbaz Gerriau dro tho Carnoak* — A few words about Cornish. R Morton Nance, the Cornish scholar, has claimed that it was Nicholas who wrote the text and not his son. So far there is little evidence to substantiate this. In this study Boson writes that Cornish was 'only spoken from Land's End to the Mount and towards St Ives, and Redruth and again from Lizard towards Helston and Falmouth'.

Scholars claim that Nicholas was the author of what is perhaps the oldest folk tale written in Cornish — *Jowan Chy an Hor* — John of Chyanhor. Edward Lhuyd, the eminent Celtic scholar who first published the tale, said it was written about 1667. A portion of the manuscript Lhuyd copied, found among manuscripts in the British Museum, was in John Boson's handwriting. The story of *Jowan Chy an Hor* is a popular tale, of a labouring man who lived at St Levan and who travels eastwards seeking work. An English version was printed in *Blackwood's Magazine* in 1818 whilst another was also printed in an early volume of *Chambers' Journal* but described as an Irish folk tale! John Boson carried on a correspondence with his friend William Gwavas entirely in Cornish. Gwavas, born in 1676, became a barrister in London, and was a lay preacher at Paul, near Penzance. He collected a large number of Cornish manuscripts which eventually passed into the hands of the British Museum, a collection that is now invaluable.

Thomas Tonkin, another member of this group of scholars, collected a large number of Cornish folk songs and sayings. Tonkin was a tailor in St Just. Of original work in Cornish, Tonkin is famous for the song about James II and William of Orange beginning *Menja toz kernuak buz galowes* . . . The song consists of 14 four line stanzas, the music, as well as words, being Celtic. It was from Edward Chirgwin, *circa* 1698, that Tonkin collected songs like *Pela era why moaz, moz, fettow teag* . . .? well known in English as 'Where are you going, my pretty maid?' Cornwall, like Wales, was certainly not lagging behind in the world of song. Carew in his *Survey of Cornwall,* wrote that Cornish, like Welsh and Breton, lent itself well to singing.

Despite this literary activity, Bishop Gibson remarks in his edition of *Britannia,* 1695, that the *Pascon agan Arluth* and the *Ordinalia* were the only pieces of literature in Cornish. Gibson's work contains a short history of Cornish, the Lord's Prayer and the Creed. Seventeenth century scholars had tried to save the Cornish language from death by giving it something which had not existed before — an extensive literature. Generally their works have little literary merit but at least they provided some examples of the latter stages of the language's development.

5   The Decline

The eighteenth century was the last in which the Cornish language was in general use. It is a fact to be wondered at that it had survived 800 years after Cornwall's conquest. During the latter half of the seventeenth century it can safely be assumed that there were few monoglot Cornish speakers left. A woman called Cheston Marchant of Gwithian died in 1676, aged 64. It is recorded that she spoke no other language but Cornish, showing that it was strange to find someone who was not bilingual at the time.

The absence of a thriving literature in the language — such as there was in Welsh — made Cornish as a tongue seem unimportant. Among

17

the Cornish there was a diminished feeling or sentiment of national consciousness. In fact, it could be said that the majority of Cornish people suffered from apathy and inferiority with regard to their nationality, because they were losing their roots in history. They had 'aped' the English gentry to the extent they had become provincial English. Parents refused to speak Cornish with their children so that they would not be 'handicapped' by the language. And so, after 1700, the language began to decline rapidly, and one writer in 1722 claimed that at St Ives only the fishermen and miners used the language at all.

At the beginning of the eighteenth century Dr Edward Lhuyd, an eminent scholar from Wales, visited Cornwall to study the language. Lhuyd found Cornish spoken in 25 parishes as a first language. He lists St Just, Paul, Buryan, Sennen, St Leven, Morva, Sancreed, Madron, Zennor, Towednack, St Ives, Lelant, Ludgvan, Gulval and other parishes from Land's End to the Lizard. Lhuyd points out that the gentry did not speak Cornish, 'there being no need, as every Cornishman speaks English'.

Lhuyd, having contacted Keigwin and his friends, set about learning Cornish. He was a Welsh speaker who had also learnt Scottish Gaelic. In 1707 he produced a book entitled *Archaeologia Brittannia* in which was printed a Cornish grammar — the first text book ever printed on the language. Tonkin and Gwavas also helped him compile a vocabulary, though this remained unpublished until the latter part of the century. Showing his mastery of Cornish, Lhuyd wrote an Elegy on William of Orange in 1702.

Dr William Borlase published a vocabulary in 1754 which was included in a work entitled *Antiquities Historical and Monumental of Cornwall*. Borlase wrote: 'I do not pretend to be a critic in it (Cornish) but desirous of doing something very difficult — to recover a lost language.'

In 1735 Gwavas and Tonkin conducted a survey among the villages along the coast from Penzance to the Land's End. They reported that people were still using Cornish in their everyday speech. In 1746 Admiral the Hon Samuel Barrington took a Cornish sailor from Mount's Bay on a trip to Brittany. Barrington wrote to his brother, the historian Daines Barrington, that the Cornish speaking sailor had made himself readily understood by the Bretons. It was Daines Barrington who wrote an account of an interview he had with Dolly Pentreath of Mousehole, in 1768. Unwittingly, perhaps, this account gave the foundation to the now popular — but entirely erroneous — belief that Dolly Pentreath was the last speaker of Cornish.

Mousehole — pronounced Mou'zl, an old Cornish word of uncertain meaning — was certainly one of the last strongholds of the language. The church of St Paul, its parish church half a mile away, contains one of the few epitaphs in Cornish. This is to Captain Stephen Hutchin (died 1709) in the south aisle.

Barrington, during a tour of Cornwall in 1768, wanted to find someone who spoke Cornish and was directed to Dolly Pentreath. 'I desired to be introduced as a person who had laid a wager that there was no one who could converse in Cornish; upon which Dolly Pentreath spoke in an angry tone of voice for two or three minutes, and in a language which sounded very like Welsh. The hut in which she lived was in a narrow lane, opposite to two rather better cottages, at the doors of which two other women stood, who were advanced in years, and who I observed were laughing. Upon this I asked them whether she had not been abusing me, to which they answered: "Very heartily, and because I had supposed she could not speak Cornish". I then said that they must be able to talk the language, to which they answered that they could not speak it readily, but they understood it, being only 10 or 12 years younger than Dolly Pentreath.' Barrington, in 1773, reported his interview to the Society of Antiquaries who published the account in their journal in 1776.

Dolly Pentreath died a year later. Daines Barrington contributed a second paper to *Archaeologia* in 1776, containing a letter received in 1776 from a fisherman of Mousehole together with an English translation. The fisherman, William Bodener who died in 1794, says that he knew five people in Mousehole alone who spoke Cornish and this conclusively disproves the Dolly Pentreath fable. Barrington also stated that John Nancarrow of Marazion (born 1709) and who was still living in the 1790s was also a native speaker. Bodenor claimed that he and Dolly Pentreath used to have long talks in Cornish, though a man named Thompson of Truro, who was the author of Dolly Pentreath's epitaph, claimed he knew more Cornish than she did.

In 1790 one of the most interesting and exacting text books to be written on Cornish was published. This was *Archaeologia Cornu-Britannica* by Dr William Pryce. The book contains Lhuyd's Grammar, under his own name, and the copious vocabulary collected by Gwavas and Tonkin plus several Cornish texts. Prince Louis Lucien Bonaparte, a keen student of Cornish, maintained Pryce had 'unscrupulously plagiarised' it. However, Pryce, with his careful editing, did Cornish a great service for it was his books that enabled the nineteenth century scholar, Dr Edwin Norris, to gain sufficient knowledge to bring out his translation of the Middle Cornish dramas.

The expansion of industry, particularly in Cornish mining in the nineteenth century, drove the last remnants of Cornish into limbo. Towns were growing and prospering, urban communities growing out of remote rural areas. The railways and new turnpikes followed. The Cornish language had ceased to exist to the outsider. Indeed, it seemed that even Cornishmen and women had lost the very memory of it.

6 Did Cornish Die?

Did the Cornish language die at the end of the eighteenth century? It is a pertinent question. By death it is meant that native knowledge of the language ceased. We have ample evidence that there were a number of native speakers still alive in the early 1800s. But did they pass on this knowledge to their children?

John Tremethack died in 1852 aged 87. He taught Cornish to his daughter Mrs Kelynack of Newlyn who was still alive in 1875. Mrs W J Rawlings of Hayle learned to say the Lord's Prayer and Creed in Cornish at her school in Penzance. She was the mother-in-law of the Cornish scholar, Henry Jenner and died in 1879 aged 57. Bernard Victor of Mousehole learnt a great deal of Cornish from his father. Victor met Jenner in 1875 and passed on to him his knowledge of the language. Jago, in his *English-Cornish Dictionary* remarks: 'Even now there are men living (Mr Bernard Victor of Mousehole and Mr W F Pentreath of Newquay, to wit) who know many Cornish words quite apart from books; words which have been handed down and are not yet dead. Furthermore, the Cornish dialect is to this day full of Celtic Cornish words.' Victor and Pentreath listed some of their Cornish vocabulary in the Penzance newspaper *The Cornishman* in 1879. Dr Stevens of St Ives, talking to the historian John Hobson Matthews in 1892, recalled he was taught to count in Cornish. He remembered his grandfather frequently used to exclaim *Scatel angow!* which has been interpreted as 'a pack of lies!' This could well be equivalent to the Welsh *ysgafael ongou!*

Of John Davey of Zennor who died in 1891, it was claimed that he was the last surviving native speaker of the language. His stone memorial reads 'John Davey 1812-1891 of Boswednack in this parish ... who was the last to possess any traditional considerable knowledge of the Cornish language.' Davey, it was reported, could hold conversations on many topics in Cornish. He also sang various traditional Cornish songs.

It would seem, then, that there were at least a small number of Cornish who had learned the language, or phrases of it, from their parents. From this evidence it can safely be said that the last native speakers of Cornish did not die out until the end of the nineteenth century.

Cornish scholarship did not die out either. On the contrary, it appeared to flourish more than ever with a great number of text books being published on Cornish grammar. In 1826 Davies Gilbert edited Keigwin's version of *Pascon agan Arluth* and the following year edited Jordan's *Gwryans an Bys*.

The majority of Middle Cornish manuscripts were now forgotten, hidden in the British Museum or the Bodleian Library. They probably would have remained lost to posterity had it not been for the diligent research of Dr Edwin Norris and Dr Whitley Stokes. In 1859 Oxford University Press published Edwin Norris' *The Ancient Cornish Drama*, a transcription with translation of the three dramas of the *Ordinalia*. In the same year Edward Ley of Bosalian made a copy of the Keigwin version of the *Ordinalia,* the manuscript of which lies in the Bodleian Library. Whitley Stokes published *Pascon agan Arluth* in 1860-61, followed by *Gwryans an Bys* in 1864. These texts were accompanied by a rather literal English translation.

The first comprehensive Cornish dictionary was published in 1865, its author being a native Welsh speaker, Robert Williams, who had discovered the manuscript of *Bewnans Meryasek.* His work, *Lexicon Cornu-Britannicum,* is a very thorough presentation of Cornish but it appeared a few years before some ancient Cornish manuscripts were rediscovered which added 2000 new words to the vocabulary. Whitley Stokes published these a few years later as *A Cornish Glossary. Bewnans Meryasek* was published in 1872, edited and translated by Whitley Stokes. In 1866 William Copeland Borlase had published *Proverbs and Rhymes in Cornish* and in 1879 he published an edition of *Nebbez Gerriau dro tho Carnoak* with translation and notes. *A Glossary of Cornish Place Names,* compiled by Rev John Bannister, was published during the same year and proved an invaluable work.

Bannister had been working on a Cornish dictionary but died before this work was complete. It was left for his friend, Dr Frederick W P Jago, to publish his *English-Cornish Dictionary,* in 1887. It is a compilation which was the result of many years of research, but unfortunately contains a number of pseudo-Cornish and slang words.

The work of the nineteenth century scholars was of vital importance as far as current interest in the language is concerned. At the time of their publication, however, little attention was paid to their work. Only a few Welsh philologists and Celtic scholars found them of interest. Cornish, by the close of the nineteenth century was generally accepted as dead; in fact the general public had forgotten that there had ever been such a thing as a Cornish language. After the passing of the 1870 Education Act, Cornish history was no longer taught in schools and children in the county were brought up with no knowledge of their Celtic past.

Conditions in Cornwall had taken a sudden downward plunge and a depression had set in by the middle of the nineteenth century. The mining industry was no longer profitable, for England could now command a vast empire and it was cheaper to get tin or copper from abroad. An agricultural depression in 1874 worsened matters whilst the fishing industry became a 'free for all'. In 1870 there were 1260 boats and 2460 men engaged in drifting alone: by the beginning of the twentieth century the entire Cornish fishing fleet numbered only 420 boats and 820 men. The old Cornish toast *Pysk, Sten ha Cober!* (Fish, Tin and Copper) was no longer heard. By 1920 a new toast had replaced it: 'China clay and Tourists!'

7   The Revivalists

The idea of Cornish becoming a living language again was an absurd thought at the beginning of the twentieth century. A very few Cornish scholars knew the language and all the native speakers had died out. Cornwall to all intents and purposes had become merely an English county.

But one man had the idea of there being a living Cornish language again. Henry Jenner saw his fellow Cornishmen in total ignorance of their heritage and their history; troubled by the Celtic spirit within them but with no outlet for it. He decided to provide Cornishmen with the incentive and the means of returning to being Cornish in speech as well as name. Jenner's reason was stated in his work *A Handbook of the Cornish Language,* published in 1904. 'Why should Cornishmen learn Cornish? There is no money in it, it serves no practical purpose, and the literature is scanty and of no great originality or value. The question is a fair one, the answer is simple. Because they are Cornish.'

Jenner was born at St Columb Major in 1848, a brilliant scholar who read a paper to the Philological Society in 1873 on 'The Cornish Language'. This excellent study was published in 1893. He then read a paper to the British Archaeological Society meeting in Penzance in August 1876, entitled 'The History and Literature of the Ancient

Cornish Language'. This created a great interest among British scholars, few of whom realised the existence of any Cornish language. This paper was published in the Society's journal the following year. Jenner, who held a post in the British Museum, made an important discovery while researching there in 1877. On the back of an old charter dated 1340 he found 41 lines of Cornish verse, a fragment of an old play, written around 1400. This added a most important piece of Middle Cornish drama to the fragments that remained.

Jenner spent much time touring Cornwall, interviewing people who still remembered the language and collecting vocabulary, songs and phrases. In this work he was encouraged by his wife, the Cornish novelist Kitty Lee. In December 1877, Jenner organised a memorial ceremony for Dolly Pentreath in order to draw attention to the language. The Bishop of Truro surprised everyone by sending a message of congratulations to the ceremony in Cornish. The Breton editor of the *Revue Celtique* also sent a message. Jenner had become proficient in Breton as well as Cornish and was admitted as a Bard of the Breton Gorsedd, founded in 1901, under the Bardic name of *Gwaz Mikael* (Servant of Michael). In 1901 Jenner instigated the formation of *Cowethas Kelto-Kernuak* — the Celtic Cornish Society — the first Cornish language movement.

Two years later Jenner attended the Congress of the Union Regionaliste Bretonne at Lesneven, Finistere, where he made a speech in Cornish to those attending. This was the first time the language had been heard on a public platform probably for centuries yet the Bretons understood the speech. The following year Jenner took Cornwall's application for membership of the Celtic Congress to their meeting at Caernarvon. While delegates listened with interest to Jenner's lecture on the Cornish language, many opposed his plea on the grounds that Cornwall was no longer Celtic. On a vote the Congress did, however, accept Cornwall's membership. Jenner was also successful in asking that Cornishmen proficient in Cornish be admitted to the Gorsedd of Wales at Llangollen.

The secretary of *Cowethas Kelto-Kernuak* now suggested to Jenner that interest in Cornish was growing so much there was need for a popular textbook that would give a summary of the language and enable Cornishmen to learn it in an easy fashion. In 1904 Jenner's *Handbook* proved to be the turning point for the revival of interest in the language. One Cornishman to start learning the language through Jenner's book was Robert Morton Nance, one of the most important leaders of the revivalists. Born in Cardiff in 1873 of Cornish parents, he and Jenner began to correspond in Cornish in 1909. Slowly the group of Cornish enthusiasts began to grow but it was Jenner, Morton Nance,

Richard Hall of St Just-in-Penwith, W D Watson and R St V Allin-Collins who really revived conversational Cornish. Allin-Collins was a professional translator in London and became a prolific writer of short stories in Cornish. By his own example as a fluent speaker he banished the idea that Cornish was a dead language that could not be saved. But the language was spelt phonetically and there were many discrepancies in spelling. The subject occupied Morton Nance and he set to work to find a unified system of spelling based on the surviving Cornish literature, particularly Middle Cornish texts, as well as on philological and phonetical grounds. It took him years of study and testing before he was successful in producing a unified spelling system which has facilitated the learning of Cornish.

Cowethas Kelto-Kernuak lapsed during the First World War years but, in 1920, Morton Nance and Jenner founded the first old Cornwall Society at St Ives. The motto of the Society was *Cuntelleugh an brewyon us gesys na vo kellys travyth* — Gather ye the fragments that are left that nothing be lost. The aim of the Society was the preservation of all that is Celtic in Cornwall, especially the language. By 1970 there were 33 Old Cornwall societies in the Duchy, constituting the Federation of Old Cornwall Societies.

With the language revival gathering momentum, Jenner decided the time was ripe, in 1928, to institute a Cornish Gorsedd bringing together those who had the revival of Cornish at heart. On September 21 the first Gorsedd Kernow was held at Boscawen-un, near St Buryan, with Jenner as the Grand Bard of Cornwall. The ceremony has been held every year since then. Bards are admitted to the Gorsedd Kernow when they have been adjudged worthy for the work they have done in the arts, music, literature, historical or archaeological work. Bards are particularly admitted for their work for the Cornish language and if they have passed three exacting examinations in Cornish which they may not take in less than two successive yearly sittings.

In 1929, the year following the first Gorsedd, Morton Nance published *Cornish For All* embodying his unified system of spelling: henceforward students adopted his instructions on phonology, spelling and pronunciation.

In 1930 A S D Smith, a schoolmaster from Sussex who had become a Welsh bard and had written a textbook *Welsh Made Easy,* learnt Cornish through Lewis' *Llawlyfr Cernyweg Canol* published in 1923. Smith, an exceptional linguist, was teaching in Cornwall at the time and started to give instruction to a class of interested boys. By 1931 the progress of this class inspired Smith to produce a book entitled *Lessons in Spoken Cornish.* Smith was convinced, because of the progress of his pupils, that Cornish could be revived as a generally spoken language. Jenner had already approached the education authorities in the County in 1930 on the idea of introducing Cornish as an optional subject in local schools. But the authorities were cynical and refused to consider the suggestion. A Celtic Congress was held in Truro in 1932 at which eight Cornish bards delivered talks in Cornish. The highlight of the Congress was the performance of a play *An Balores,* the Chough, by Morton Nance. The next year the first Cornish national movement with a political interest was formed. This was known as *Tyr ha Tavas,* Land and Language, under the leadership of Dr E H Hambly. *Tyr ha Tavas* was a pressure group which approached MPs and pointed out wrongs in Cornwall. The movement marked a tremendous change in the Cornish attitude. No longer apathetic, people were beginning to awake to a sense of Celtic nationality again. *Tyr ha Tavas* instigated an annual church service in Cornish, first held on Sunday 27 August 1933, at Towednack. Landewednack was the parish church where the last Cornish services were preached in 1678.

A move to accommodate the growing demand for Cornish classes was made in 1933 by the Federation of Old Cornwall Societies which opened new classes in seven towns. Cornish was now accepted as part of the curriculum for Celtic studies. In 1934, at the age of 86, Henry Jenner, 'Father of the Cornish Language Revival', died. He had seen his dream in 1873 becoming a reality. Cornwall was becoming aware of its Cornishness once again.

8   The Growth of the Revival

The natural successor to Henry Jenner as Grand Bard of the Cornish Gorsedd was Robert Morton Nance and in September 1934 he was installed in office at Padderbury Top, Liskeard. In that year the publication of an *English-Cornish Dictionary* fulfilled a widely felt need for such a work. The dictionary was the result of a collaboration between Morton Nance and A S D Smith. The latter launched in 1933 a monthly magazine called *Kernow,* written entirely in Cornish. This was an immediate success and found subscribers in twelve countries.

In 1935, as has already been stated, the BBC broadcast a programme of choral music in Cornish. The programme was so popular that the BBC were induced to broadcast many other such programmes with six Cornish choirs. The revival was attracting so much attention that the London *Times* devoted a leading article to it.

In 1935 Morton Nance published what he described as his life's work — a *Cornish-English Dictionary*. Some £2000 was raised by voluntary donations for the publication of this epic work which has been described as the most modern work on Cornish in existence. While the war years stopped the public ceremonies of the Gorsedd Kernow it in no way stopped the publication of works in Cornish. In 1939 A S D Smith had produced a complete grammar of the language with exercises called *Cornish Simplified*. This has been reprinted many times since and has become one of the standard works for students. During the same year Morton Nance published *Lyver an Pymp Marthus Seleven* — Book of the Five Miracles of Seleven, a folk lore tale of a Cornish saint. An intriguing aspect of the war years was the correspondence between Smith and Edwin Chirgwin, who had published 240 conversational pieces on everyday topics in Cornish and English in 1937 entitled *Say it in Cornish*. Chirgwin was stationed in Gibraltar as was E G Retallack Hooper, and the three men conducted a correspondence in Cornish. Whenever they sent a letter they had to send an English translation with it so that it could pass the official censor.

With the war over, the Cornish Gorsedd resumed its public meetings at Perran Round. Interest in Cornish began to increase greatly and the education authorities realised the need to provide for this growing demand. Evening classes were started at Falmouth and St Austell in addition to those by the Federation of Old Cornwall Societies. An annual summer school *Scol haf Kernewek* was also instituted at St Brandon's School, Truro.

In 1950 A S D Smith died, a great loss to the revivalist movement. Following the war he had produced several more works in Cornish as well as a pamphlet on *How to learn Cornish*. By far the greatest work was *Trystan hag Ysolt,* published in 1951 by his widow as a memorial volume.

With the re-awakening of the Cornish language had come a re-awakening of Cornish nationhood. On 31 December 1932 the *Western Morning News* reported a speech of Henry Jenner in which he used the phrase *'bedheugh byntha Kernewek!'* (Be forever Cornish!) A group of young men and women, enthused by the language revival, formed Cornwall's first national political movement under the name *Tyr ha Tavas* (Land and Language). They became a pressure group lobbying Parliament. In April 1934 the magazine *Kernow* was launched, edited by A S D Smith, as the official journal of the movement. *Tyr ha Tavas* became moribund during the 1939-45 period and was replaced for a short while by a group called Young Cornwall.

On 5 January 1951, Cornishmen and women came together at Redruth to launch a new movement called Mebyon Kernow (Sons of Cornwall). Their initial aim was 'to maintain the character of Cornwall as a Celtic nation, to promote the interests of Cornwall and the Cornish people and to promote the constitutional advance of Cornwall and its right to self-government in domestic affairs'.

Mebyon Kernow's policy towards the Cornish language revival was that, while recognising Cornwall must continue to use English as a medium, 'learning Cornish must be an option available to each child, with other languages, all equally provided with means, equipment, books and teachers. Cornish must be given examination status.'

In May 1964 Mebyon Kernow revised its aims. These were now 'to maintain the Celtic character of Cornwall and its right to self-government in domestic affairs, to foster the Cornish language, literature, culture and sport and to demand that Cornish children have the opportunity in school to learn about their own land and culture.' From a pressure group, Mebyon Kernow now made the change to being a political party with candidates standing firstly in local government elections. In 1967 Colin Murley was elected as Mebyon Kernow's first county councillor for St Day/Lanner on the Cornwall County Council. Other election successes followed in rural and district councils. In 1970 Richard Jenkin stood as Mebyon Kernow's first parliamentary candidate for Falmouth-Camborne, receiving 960 votes.

Some Cornish nationalists felt that Mebyon Kernow's aim of domestic self-government was not adequate for the needs of Cornwall. A split occurred in Mebyon Kernow and in June 1969, Leonard C Trelease, a former national secretary of Mebyon Kernow, established a Cornish National Party demanding Commonwealth Status for an independent Cornwall. Robert Holmes, who had won a seat on Liskeard council for Mebyon Kernow, switched his allegiance to the new party and became its leader. In May 1975, the party became the Cornish Nationalist Party. When, in 1979, it put forward its first parliamentary candidate, its aims had been modified to 'regional status within the United Kingdom, within Europe'.

As the language revival had given birth to a revival of political nationalism, so now did the political movement engender new life in the language movement.

In January 1952, Richard Gendall, a language teacher, launched an all-Cornish magazine called *An Lef* (The Voice) which was designed to fill the gap left by the demise of Smith's *Kernow*. Designed as a monthly, after the tenth issue E G R 'Talek' Hooper took over the editorship and it later took the title of *An Lef Kernewek*. It appeared quarterly until 1984. Gendall launched another magazine in May 1956, entitled *Hedhyu* (Today) which ceased publication in 1961. He was also involved with Richard Jenkin in launching a mainly English language periodical *New Cornwall.*

The continued growth of the revival caused the establishment of *Kesva an Tavas Kernewek* (The Cornish Language Board) in November 1967. *An Kesva* took over all aspects of the revivalist movement, conducting examinations to GCE level. *An Kesva* was endorsed by the Gorseth Kernow and by the Cornwall Education Committee. The first general secretary was P A S Pool, whose textbook *Cornish for Beginners* became a popular work. One of the most influential work for teachers and learners of this period was undoubtedly Gendall's *Kernewek Bew* (Living Cornish), published in 1972. At the time, it was regarded as the 'last word' in teaching manuals.

In 1979 *An Kesva* instigated an associate membership under the title *Cowethas an Yeth Kernewek* (The Cornish Language Fellowship). *Cowethas* took over responsibility for the publication of a monthly magazine *An Gannas* (The Ambassador) launched in December 1976. The magazine is entirely in Cornish and since the demise of *An Lef Kernewek,* after 32 years of publication, *An Gannas* is now the premier Cornish language periodical.

In 1984 *Cowethas* published *Kernewek Hedhya: Deryvas War Stuth an Tavas,* a bilingual report on the state of the language. The report revealed that five primary schools and two secondary schools in Cornwall were teaching Cornish as an optional subject.

One of the most significant and exciting developments was the birth of *Dalleth* (Beginning). By the end of the 1970s it was seen that despite the ever-increasing facilities for the learning, practice and use of Cornish, the activities were organised with adults in mind. To revive a language one needs young speakers. In October 1979 *Dalleth* was launched with the aim of publishing children's books and promoting opportunities for children of all ages to learn the language, including the establishment of a playschool group. *Dalleth* launched a children's monthly *Len ha Lyw.* Regular playschool groups were organised but were difficult to sustain. Those parents interested in Cornish playschool groups lived scattered throughout Cornwall and it was difficult to bring them together on a regular basis. It was also noticed that one of the problems with children who learned Cornish at home and in the playgroup was that they tended to reject the language when moving on to a primary school, where they nearly always found a hostile English-speaking environment. *Dalleth* began to concentrate on publications and on encouraging teachers to introduce Cornish culture in its widest sense into schools, producing cassettes of nursery songs and rhymes in the language.

In 1987 a new group *Agan Tavas* (Our Language) was formed with the specific purpose of promoting Cornish as a spoken means of communication among the young.

In 1984 in addition to the seven schools providing Cornish language classes as an optional subject, there were eighteen classes being held in various Cornish centres with five more evening classes in other parts of the United Kingdom plus a *Kernewek dre Lyther* (Cornish by Post) correspondence school attracting learners from many parts of the world.

There was no lack of publications in Cornish. Apart from publications from *An Kesva* and others, Dyllansow Truran of Redruth, run by Len Truran, became the main Cornish language publisher. The company had done, and continues to do, much sterling work in supplying the demand for books about or in the language. In 1984 Dyllansow Truran made history by publishing the first full-length novel in Cornish, a political thriller entitled *An Gurun Wosek a Geltya* (The Bloody Crown of Celtia) by Melville Bennetto.

The summer of 1987 saw *An Gresen Gernewek* (The Cornish Language Centre) established near Truro. There is a regular Cornish language programme broadcast weekly on Radio Cornwall. In April 1984 Cornwall submitted two films in Cornish at the Fifth Celtic Film and Television Festival, held in Cardiff, Wales. These were the first Cornish language films ever made: *Jowan Chy an Horth,* directed by Sarah Stuart Wood for Begville Enterprises and *An Canker Seth* (The Crab Pot) directed by J Phillips for Television Southwest Ltd.

Whereas since the commencement of the language revival, the movement had received, until 1988, no grants, endowments or other official encouragement, grants were made at the end of that year. The European Economic Community's Bureau for Lesser Used Languages gave an endowment to *An Kesva*. Subsequently a similar grant was made by the Cornwall County Council.

The success of the Cornish Language Revival had caused Professor Chaim Rabin, Professor of Hebrew at the Hebrew University of Jerusalem, to state: 'The revival of Cornish is the only true parallel to the Hebrew case.' Hebrew, of course, was revived as the official language of the state of Israel some 2000 years after it had ceased to be a generally spoken language.

However, in 1988 problems began to emerge in the revivalist movement. In fact, the Cornish Language Revival had become the victim of its own success.

9 Cornish: Present and Future

What was once a homogenous revival movement has today split into three main camps. Until 1988 the official orthography of Cornish was the system devised by Robert Morton Nance (1873-1959). He had realised that there was a need for a standard spelling to assist learners. He rejected Late Cornish (1650-1800) with its high admixture of English borrowings and turned to the Middle Cornish texts of the 14-16th centuries as a 'purer' form of the language and used them to create his standard orthography. Where words were missing from the surviving Middle Cornish, he borrowed forms peculiar to Late Cornish and sometime synthesised words from Welsh and Breton equivalents. The resultant system, first introduced in his book *Cornish For All,* 1929, was called Unified Cornish.

Unified Cornish has been criticised on a number of levels. Not the least, it has been totally rejected by the world of Celtic scholarship as not reflective of the Cornish language at any stage of its spoken history. Some Celtic scholars, such as Dr Glanville Price, take the view that it is a synthetic language. The same observation can be made about several revived languages, particularly Hebrew in which grammatical reconstructions and a new vocabulary to express modern concepts are decided by the Academy of the Hebrew Language and made law by Government.

But with the increasing demands on the Cornish language as a vehicle of modern expression, above all as a means of verbal expression, and lacking a permanent body of linguistic experts to make amendments from time to time on the Hebrew model, the Unified system became the subject of increasing concern because of the inconsistencies beween the spoken and written word resulting in variations in pronunciation of a considerable proportion of the language. As Cornish speakers gained proficiency, they inevitably returned to the original texts and all too often discovered that the Unified system gave a less than useful guide to pronunciation.

As early as 1972, Cornishman Tim Saunders, a graduate in Celtic studies from Aberystwyth, criticised the Unified system, pointing out these flaws. In the early 1980s Richard Gendall, a language teacher and author of one of the best-known textbooks on the language — *Kernewek Bew* (Living Cornish) approached Kesva an Tavas Kernewek proposing that the criticisms be taken seriously and a study made on the subject. An Kesva rejected Gendall's proposal and he appeared to drop out of the language movement.

In 1986 Dr Ken George, education officer of Cowethas an Yeth Kernewek, a graduate of Brest in Brittany, with a fluency both in Unified Cornish and Breton and with a good working knowledge of Welsh, published his study *Pronunciation and Spelling of Revised Cornish*. Dr George had previously outlined some of the problems of Unified in *A Phonological History of Cornish*, 1984. He set about tackling the problems using a computer to attempt to define the sounds of the language as they supposedly were in the 15/16th centuries. On this basis he proposed a new spelling system, a phonemic system, to fit more closely the spoken language. His main thesis was that Middle Cornish should continue to be the basis of the language of the modern revival as it was in the Unified system. He made a closely argued review of the phonemes of Middle Cornish based on a computerised analysis of all the surviving literary evidence.

Kesva an Tavas Kernewek gave serious consideration to Dr George's new system and in the autumn of 1987 announced that it was adopting the system — Phonemic Cornish. In the summer of 1988 the Gorseth Kernow agreed that submissions to the Gorseth competitions could be made either in Unified or in Phonemic. The principle of a change from Unified to Phonemic was accepted and, while a three year period was mentioned, no decision was agreed on a time scale.

This decision was greeted with dismay by a large section of Unified enthusiasts. Richard Jenkin, a former Grand Bard of the Cornish Gorsedd (1976-82) became one of the leading spokesmen for the Unified school. Whilst admitting some amendments to the Unified system were needed, he rejected Dr George's Phonemic system as Breton-influenced and proposing a system of spelling foreign to Cornish. Indeed, Dr George has felt compelled to amend several of his proposals. In his system, the Cornish word for house 'Chy' would have been rendered 'Tji'. While this would have given a close phonemic rendering it did present a word foreign in appearance to historical Cornish orthography. Dr George has now re-adopted 'Chy'.

Richard Gendall, in the meantime, had not been lost to the revivalist movement. After his rebuff from An Kesva he had set about dealing with the problem in his own way. He had come to the conclusion that the only way forward was to pick up Cornish in the state it had been at the time of its death — Late Cornish, the language of 1650-1800, or as Gendall called it, *Cornoack*, Traditional Cornish.

According to Gendall: 'Traditional Cornish is the vernacular tongue as it survived latest.' Gendall's studies in this field have attracted interest from some scholars who view it as being reflective of the Cornish language at an historical period. However, to make Late Cornish a basis for a revival of the language, a great deal of work would need to be done, especially to ensure the language's viability for modern expression. Gendall and his wife have established a cultural centre at Menheniot called Teere ha Tavaz (Land and Language) and have began to produce a series of textbooks and tapes in Late Cornish; these include *Deen Ahanan* (Let's Go), a comprehensive work conceived as a replacement for Gendall's Unified learner *Kernewek Bew*. *Cowz an Ewhel* (Speak *up!*), a direct method course using illustrations and cassettes, had also been published. An all-Cornish quarterly *Teere ha Tavaz* is also produced.

In April 1989 Rod Lyon, a leading figure in the language movement, produced a booklet *Authentic Cornish*. Rod Lyon persuasively argued that as Unified had been a vibrant vehicle of the language revival for the last fifty years, it should not be abandoned so readily. He felt that the orthography of Late Cornish could 'incorporate a corrected Unified spelling, with all the mistakes, anomalies and omissions of Nance having been erased'.

At the moment *An Gannas* (The Ambassador), the monthly Cornish language publication, supports the change to the Phonemic system. A new publication *Delyow Derow* (Oakleaves) seeks to maintain the Unified system. And *Teere ha Tavaz* (Land and Language) promotes the Late Cornish or Cornoack system. If the language revival is going to continue with the same success as in recent decades it is obvious that one form of orthography must be agreed upon. Cornish has come to a crossroads and decisions taken in the next few years will be crucial to the future of the language. The answer rests with the Cornish people.

And to those who ask the inevitable question 'Why should Cornishmen and women learn Cornish?', it is Henry Jenner, as Father of the Revival, who still supplies the most simple answer: 'Because they are Cornish!'

For further information on Cornish contact:

Unified
Dyllansow Truran, Trewolsta, Trewirgie, Redruth, Cornwall.

Phonemic
Kesva an Tavas Kernewek (Cornish Language Board), 'Chy-an-Gell', 9 Frith Road, Saltash, Cornwall.

Traditional
Teere ha Tavaz, Tregrill Vean, Menheniot, Liskeard PL14 3PL, Cornwall.